SOLITUDE & REBIRTH

"Failure halts your steps,
but solitude sets your soul in motion again."

by
BUTTERFLYMAN

ButterflyMan Publishing LLC

For permission requests, contact:

ButterflyMan Publishing LLC

Email: **contact@butterflyman.com**

Website: **www.butterflyman.com**

This book is a work of nonfiction.

All analysis, interpretations, and frameworks are the author's own.

First Edition — 2025

Printed in the United States of America

ISBN: 979-8-90217-008-2

Book Design: **ButterflyMan Publishing LLC**

Table of Contents

Chapter 0 · Success and Failure: Two Sides of the Same Coin 9

Chapter 1 — When You Fail, You Just Fail: Stop Punishing Yourself 31

Chapter 2 — How to Begin Again: 39

Chapter 3— Business Failure & Relationship Failure: 46

Chapter 4 — Preparing for Failure: 56

Chapter 5 Living Alone: 64

Chapter 6: Reevaluating Your "Invisible Assets" 72

Chapter 7: Relearning: Rebuilding Yourself Through Books, Skills, and Buddhist Wisdom 79

Chapter 8 — Rebuilding the Way You Live: Living Calm and Unmoved 87

Chapter 9 — Keep Moving in Your Field: 94

Chapter 10 — Silence Is Gold: The Final Lesson of Rebirth 101

Epilogue — May You Meet Yourself Again in the Quiet 108

Foreword

I have worked for forty years, and thirty-three of those were spent building and running my own companies.
Along this journey, success and failure intertwined again and again.
Some failures pushed me all the way to the bottom—left with nothing, relying on help from family and friends just to get through each day.
Sometimes the struggle lasted a year or two; sometimes five or six.
Each time, the impact on my family was heavy and painful.

No matter how strong-minded or disciplined a person may be, reality remains harsh.
Especially in the United States, where everyone lives independently and carries their own burdens, few people have the surplus energy or resources to support another person for long.

That is why one must be cautious—
You cannot let idealism push you into the fire like a moth rushing toward the flame.
Yet, on the other hand, without courage, no one can break open a new path.
Balancing these two forces is the hardest part of life.
Too much courage becomes recklessness;
Too much caution becomes paralysis.
A slight misalignment can lead to devastating failure.

Once failure happens, there is only one thing a person can do:
Retreat, recover, and slowly rebuild.
It is easy to say "never give up,"
But anyone who has endured pressure, debt, shame, or desperation knows—
It is a daily battle with oneself.
Reality magnifies fear;
The mind magnifies pain;
And the weight of both can feel unbearable.

No one wishes for failure, yet failure is a common state of life.

During one of my most difficult periods, an older friend—originally from Hong Kong and later settled in the United States—shared with me four unforgettable words:
"A dead horse keeps walking." （死馬前行）
That spirit has stayed with me ever since.
It is also one of the defining qualities of Hong Kong people:
Even at rock bottom, they still push forward.

In my hometown in China, we had a wooden spinning top when I was a child—

Oval-shaped with a sharp tip at the bottom.
You had to pull a string sharply to make it spin, and then keep striking it with a small whip to maintain its motion.
We called it *"the indestructible Li Kui."*

It would fall and spin out,
But with one more strike, it would rise and whirl again.
Years later, a senior who knew me well told me:
"You are exactly that Li Kui."
The moment I heard it, something stirred deeply within me.
It was, in fact, the most accurate description of who I am.

Tonight, after dinner and an evening walk, I felt an impulse to sit down and write this foreword—
To gather the experiences of my life,
The failures I have endured,
The solitude I have walked through,
And the rebirths I have found within it all.
If even one part of these reflections can help someone who is facing their own darkness,
Then this writing has meaning.

Life is unpredictable.
At some point, everyone will fall into solitude.
If these words can offer you direction or strength when you are at your lowest,
Then they have fulfilled their purpose.

ButterflyMan
New York
November 2025

Book Outline

Prologue | Solitude: The Doorway Back to Yourself

Solitude is not a punishment.
It is a chance to rebuild.
All rebirth happens in quietness, not in crowds.

Chapter 0   Success & Failure: Two Sides of the Same Coin

Success is not eternal light,
and failure is not the final darkness.
What matters is learning to let go of both,
come back to yourself,
and begin again.

Chapter 1   Failure Is Just Failure—Stop Punishing Yourself

- Failure does *not* require "analysis"
- It is not philosophy, not fate
- It is simply failure
- Don't let it bind you
- No regret, no made-up narratives
- The only meaning of failure: it gives you a chance to start again

Chapter 2   How to Restart: Adjust Your Mind, Take One Action

- Don't make big plans in the low point
- Choose one action you *can* do
- Small victories matter more than big goals
- Each action is a stone thrown into your future

Chapter 3   Failure in Work & Love: Let Time Wash It Away

- Work failure: recover losses, preserve cash
- Love failure: no explaining, no chasing, no entanglement
- Let time wash away what time can wash away
- What truly matters: you are still here

Chapter 4   Preparing for Failure: The Philosophy of the Survival Line

- At least 12 months of living expenses
- Never borrow high-interest money
- Never harm the future to save the present
- Better to break than to sink your next life chapter
- Financial bottom line = life bottom line

Chapter 5   During Solitude: Rebuild Yourself with Minimal Living

- Simplify life
- No smoking, no drinking, no drugs
- Stay home, reset your mind and body
- Buy nothing except necessities
- Solitude is healing; time alone is priceless

Chapter 6   Re-evaluate Your "Invisible Assets"

- What do you still have?
- Connections? Skills? Industry knowledge? Specialized expertise?
- Widen your market scope
- Rebuild relationships
- Take big and small opportunities alike
- Become a person who can earn again

Chapter 7   Learn Again: From Books, Skills, and Buddhist Texts

- Mature people save themselves through learning
- Don't pray—*read*
- No forced meditation—just quiet the heart
- Explore new tools, new fields, new worlds
- Every new learning is a new life

Chapter 8   Rebuild Your Way of Being: Calm as Always

- Don't listen to slander
- Don't argue, don't debate
- Stay away from conflict
- Be humble, be courteous

- Don't invite trouble
- Solitude is the period when character is rebuilt
- Become a *steady* person, not a *hard* person

Chapter 9   Keep Moving in Your Profession: The World Belongs to Movers

- Even after failing—keep moving
- Look at details
- Go to factories, markets, exhibitions, real sites
- Attend global trade shows
- Life begins to turn only when *you move*

Chapter 10   Silence Is Gold: The Final Lesson of Rebirth

- Don't show off, don't explain, don't announce
- Work quietly
- Don't give others weapons
- Leave space for yourself
- Silence is the strongest shield for those who are rebuilding

Epilogue | May You Meet Yourself Again in Solitude

Solitude is not punishment—
solitude is an invitation.

In that quiet place,
you will finally hear
the voice you never truly listened to before:
your own.

Chapter 0 · Success and Failure: Two Sides of the Same Coin

1. A Two-Sided Life: Success and Failure Were Never Two Different Worlds

Most people imagine life like this:
there are two parallel roads—the road of success and the road of failure.

Successful people, you think, walk on the bright road.
Failures walk on the dark road.
As long as you choose the "right" one at the beginning,
you believe you can stand in the light forever.

But anyone who has really walked far enough in life
eventually discovers something very different:

>Success and failure are not two separate roads.
>They are simply two kinds of weather on the same road.

>When the sky is clear, you think you are strong.
>When the storm hits, you think you are useless.

>But you are neither the clear sky nor the storm.
>You are just the person who keeps walking along the road.

>Success tricks you into believing you're in control of everything.
>Failure tricks you into believing you have nothing at all.

>The truth of life is in neither extreme.
>What really matters is just this:

>Whether you are at the peak or in the valley,
>do you keep walking?

>To keep walking when you're successful—that is humility.
>To keep walking when you've failed—that is courage.

>The person who can keep moving in both moments
>is the one who is truly strong.

2. Why Success Is Not Worth Getting Too Proud About

Most so-called "success" in this world
is not the sign of absolute superiority or talent.

It is more often:

>"The timing was right, the opportunity arrived,
>the direction happened to fit, and the right people appeared."

>You feel like you did everything perfectly.
>But in reality, it may simply be that the pieces of the puzzle
>happened to click together at that moment.

>Success inflates people.
>It distorts their judgment,
>and makes them think:

>"I am special. I am chosen."

>But look closely at those who truly stand at the top for a long time:
>they almost never indulge in their success.
>In fact, they are afraid—
>afraid that success will trap them.

>Because they know:

>Success is not your "essence".
>It is only your current state.

>The moment you turn success into your entire identity—
>you quietly begin to die at that point.

>You think you've reached the finish line,
>while the world keeps moving forward without you.

>The most dangerous part of success is not just pride.
>The real danger is this:

>You stop moving,
>and build a permanent camp
>on a small hill that was only meant

to be a rest stop.

3. Why Failure Is Not Worth Drowning In

Most people's first reaction to failure is collapse.

"I'm useless."
"The world is unfair."
"Fate is picking on me."

But what is the real meaning of failure?

It is a reminder:
- Perhaps your direction is not right.
- Perhaps your method needs to be adjusted.
- Perhaps you simply were not ready yet.

Failure is not the end of the world.
Failure is a stop sign.

It forces you to pause,
to give you a chance to turn around
and look at who you really are.

Most failures do not happen
because you "didn't work hard enough".

More often, they happen because:

"You worked very hard—but in the wrong direction."

Failure is like a yellow light:

"Your energy needs to be redistributed."
"Your approach needs to be re-examined."
"Your life structure needs to be reorganized."

Failure is not a verdict on your value.
It is a gentle knock on the door of your direction.

You are not "a failure".
You are just standing at a point
where adjustment has become necessary.

4. When You Fail, Don't Cling to Buddha—Come Back to Yourself

When people fail,
they have a strong urge to run away.

Run into religion,
run into fatalism,
run into excuses,
run into alcohol, drugs, and all kinds of anesthesia.

But none of these things will truly save you.
They only delay the moment you finally wake up.

You said something incredibly powerful:

> "When you fail, don't run to cling to Buddha.
> Instead, go and look for your real self."

This sentence could be printed on the cover of this book.

Praying is not bad.
But dependency is dangerous.

Religion is not the enemy.
The real enemy is escape.

When failure happens,
you don't actually need an external power
to repaint your pain in a pretty color.

What you really need is:

To pick up your own strength again.

Failure tears off your masks.
It is the most brutally honest moment of your life.

In that moment,
you can ask yourself ten questions you usually avoid:
- What do I really want to do?
- Am I holding onto a dream,
or just clinging to old inertia?
- Am I living off other people's approval?
- Am I living too exhausted?
- What exactly am I afraid of?
- What am I running away from?
- What part of myself have I refused to face for years?
- How long have I been living for others instead of for myself?
- Have I been acting out the version of "me"
that others expect, instead of my own?
- Do I still have the courage to start over now?

These questions will almost never appear
when you are successful.

They rarely surface
when life feels stable and comfortable.

Only when you drop into the dark,
do you finally see who you really are.

At that moment,
you don't need a statue of Buddha in front of you.

You need honesty—
radical honesty with yourself.

5. Loneliness: The Way You Meet Yourself Again

Loneliness is not despair.
Loneliness is a system reboot.

When a person truly enters a state of solitude,
emotions, relationships, titles, habits, roles—
they start falling off, one by one.

Your soul is finally released
from the noise of the outside world.

At last, you are able to:

Sit down at the same table as yourself.

Every real rebirth
happens in loneliness.

Anyone who has truly stood up again
has completed that process alone
in a quiet room.

Loneliness temporarily lifts you out of your social roles:

You are no longer just someone's parent,
someone's partner,
someone's employee or boss.

You are left with one identity only:

You.

Loneliness looks empty from the outside,
but inside it is completely full—
so full that you can't avoid
hearing your own inner voice.

Loneliness forces you to confront three questions:
- Who am I?
- What kind of life do I actually want?
- What am I willing to pay for that life?

These questions do not appear
in crowded social events.

They do not arise at dinners,
nor in the noise of group conversations.

They only emerge
in one person's silence.

Loneliness is not punishment.
Loneliness is an invitation—

An invitation to get to know yourself all over again.

6. After Failure, There Is Only One Thing You Really Need to Do:

Reset Your Mind, and Find One Direction You Can Move In

After failure, we tend to fall into
two major traps.

Trap #1: Trying too hard to "analyze everything"

You try to find the cause,
the person to blame,
the hidden logic,
the secret script of fate.

On the surface, this looks rational.
In reality, it often just prolongs your suffering.

The more you analyze,
the more you stay stuck in the past.

The more you "summarize",
the deeper you carve failure
into your identity.

But in life, there are many failures
that simply do not yield a clean explanation.

Failure doesn't always need
to be interpreted.

Sometimes, failure just needs
to be put down.

Trap #2: Drowning in regret

Regret is one of the most luxurious
and most useless emotions.

It does nothing but drain your energy.

It changes nothing.

You are not the failure itself.
You are simply a person
standing still for a while.

Real restart doesn't begin with thought.
It begins with movement.

After failure, you don't need big moves.
You don't need a grand new life plan.
You don't need to rebuild your entire vision overnight.

You need just one thing:

One tiny action that lets you move half a step forward.

For example:
- Clean your room.
- Delete a few contacts you truly don't need anymore.
- Write down one small task
you can begin today.
- Send one message that might lead to a new lead.
- Go for a short walk.
- Learn a skill for five minutes.
- Watch one video related to your field.

These things look trivial.
But they can carry you
from "paralyzed" to "in motion".

Life only needs one movement
to begin again.

7. Failure in Career and Failure in Love:

Let Time Wash Them Away, Instead of Letting Them Tie You Up

When your career fails,
what you lose is your outer identity.

16

When love fails,
what you lose is your emotional anchor.

The pains are different,
but the thing that heals them both
is the same:

Time.

Events will blur with time.
But if you keep squeezing your wound,
it will turn into a parasite
inside your mind.
- A collapsed business doesn't need more explanation.
- A lover who left doesn't need to be chased.
- Opportunities you missed don't need
to be replayed with endless regret.
- People who walked away don't need to be blamed.
- Broken relationships don't always need fixing.
- Being rejected, ignored, or misunderstood
doesn't always need a grand "counter-proof".

For true pain,
there is only one method:

Let time carry it away.

Your job is not to "fully understand"
or "completely forgive".
Those are results, not starting points.

What you need to do is simple:

Cut the rope with the past,
and keep your strength for the future.

Trust this:

Behind everything time washes away,
there is always a small space left behind—
a space you couldn't see back then.

That space
is the doorway to your next life chapter.

8. In a Whole Lifetime, There Is No Absolute Right,

And No Absolute Wrong

After failing, most people ask:
"What did I do wrong?"

After succeeding, most people assume:
"I must have done it right."

But whether something is "right" or "wrong"
depends, in truth, on many factors:
- Timing
- The people involved
- The situation
- The resources available
- Your mental state
- The background conditions
- What happens afterwards

A decision that looks "wrong" today
may turn out to be
the most important turning point of your life
ten years from now.

A success that looks "perfect" today
might later become the biggest weight
holding you back.

Life is not a formula.
Life is much more like the weather.

You cannot use a frozen snapshot
to judge a moving destiny.

So we have to learn:
- Not to treat success
as final proof of correctness.

- Not to treat failure
as final proof of worthlessness.
- Not to turn a single result
into a lifelong verdict.
- Not to treat any one stage
as the ultimate end.

What you need to do is always the same:

> At each moment,
> make the best decision you can
> with who you are and what you know.

> The rest belongs to time.

9. Both Success and Failure Must Be Released

Success often turns people
into victims of their own past.

You're trapped by your old achievements,
by your halo,
by everyone's expectations of you.

You forget that success is temporary,
and start believing
"this is who I am".

Failure turns people
into prisoners of their past.

You are bound by fear,
pressed down by shame,
locked up by regret.

You start believing that failure defines you,
even though it was only a moment.

You cannot stand inside success forever—
but you also do not have to sit in failure forever.

In truth, they share the same nature:

> Neither is permanent.
> But both can be your teacher—
> if you allow them to be.
>
> Life is not about
> "maintaining success at all costs"
> or "avoiding failure at all costs".
>
> Life is about this:
>
> Walking through success many times,
> walking through failure many times,
> and eventually walking back
> to yourself.
>
> Those who can let go of success
> make room to grow further.
>
> Those who can let go of failure
> make space to start again.
>
> Success is not your home.
> Failure is not your home either.
>
> Your real home
> is the road you keep choosing to walk.

10. True Strength Is Quietly Rebuilt in Silence

The world loves noise.
But real recovery always begins in quiet.

The deeper the valley,
the more you must protect your energy.

The more painful the failure,
the more you need to reduce
meaningless output.

Silence is not weakness.
Silence is you guarding yourself.
- No explaining
- No arguing
- No desperate defending
- No proving you were "right all along"
- No begging for understanding
from people who don't truly care
- No pouring your soul out
to those who don't deserve it

This is not avoidance.
This is you reclaiming your power.

Silence allows you
to store energy for your next stage.

Silence gives you space
to protect and heal yourself.

Silence helps you rebuild
your inner order.

When, in the middle of that silence,
your mind becomes clearer,
your heart becomes steadier,
and your will becomes firmer—

> You are already standing
> at the doorway of rebirth.

11. What Still Belongs to You:

Failure Shows You What You Still Have

Failure washes away
almost everything on the outside:

Status, money, relationships, connections, opportunities...
All of these can vanish very quickly.

Then you suddenly see:

Most of what you once thought
"belonged to you"
was actually on loan.
- Your position in a company is on loan.
- Most relationships are temporary.
- Many client connections vanish with circumstances.
- Love is not always guaranteed forever.
- Social identity is just a time-limited label

for one phase of your life.

When failure comes,
these things disappear at surprising speed.

But failure also shows you
what stubbornly refuses to leave:
- Your character
- Your endurance
- Your judgment
- Your specialized knowledge
- Your industry experience
- The few relationships that stayed
- Your ability to observe
- Your sensitivity to the world
- The wisdom you distilled from pain
- And the simple, stubborn will

to keep living and moving forward

These are your real assets.

Everything else is a product of circumstance.
These things are your permanent foundation.

Failure is an inventory check.

It forces you to see:

"So this is what I really have underneath everything."

12. The Season of Solitude Is the Best Time to Rebuild

Only in solitude
can a person become truly clean.

You step away from noise,
from constant judgment,
from comparisons,
from draining social obligations.

Layer by layer,
you pull out the sources of mental noise,
and finally your inner world
has some empty space again.

Solitude gives you five kinds of power.

1. Clarity: seeing what to continue and what to stop

You see which relationships are hollow.
Which dreams are real,
and which are fantasies.
Which "commitments"
are actually just habits, not true passion.

2. Filtering: cutting away what you no longer need

You sort through your phone,
your messages,
your contacts,
your daily habits,
your overstuffed schedule—

and you ask,
"Do I really need this?"

Deleting is often the first step of rebirth.

3. Reconstruction: redesigning your next life chapter

Solitude gives you time and space
to rediscover what you truly want to do—

the thing that was buried
under years of busyness and noise.

4. Depth: learning again, absorbing again, growing again

Solitude is the best season to study.

No interruptions,
fewer distractions—
your capacity to absorb
multiplies.

5. Action: discovering the power of small steps

You realize life doesn't change
through one dramatic move.

It changes through countless small steps
that, together, bring you back to shore.

Solitude purifies you.

> It slowly transforms you
> into someone who can stand
> without outer noise.

13. The Minimum Survival Line:

The Most Important Rule When You've Failed

There is one principle worth writing
into everyone's life manual:

> "Always keep at least twelve months of living expenses,
> and never touch loan sharks or predatory debt."

> This single line
> can literally save lives.

> In times of failure,
> the most dangerous thing is not

"having no money".

The most dangerous thing is:

"In order to survive now,
making choices that will destroy
your next chapter of life."

For example:
- Turning to high-interest, predatory loans
- Accepting desperate, toxic deals
- Selling yourself short
- Destroying your credit completely
- Chasing only short-term gains
- Forcing your future self
to pay for today's crisis

In seasons of failure,
you must guard three bottom lines:

1. No predatory loans. Never drink poison to quench thirst.
Loan sharks don't lend you "money";
they hand you a trap.

They are not a tool to save your future—
they are a weapon that destroys it.

2. Protect a minimum survival line. Make "safety" your core.

You don't need expansion.
You don't need big risks.
You don't need to chase every opportunity.

You just need:

A stable environment
that lets you stay alive
and reasonably sane.

3. Cut your spending to the bone. The simpler your life, the freer your mind.

Stay home more.

Cut social spending.
Stop showing off.
Stop buying things you don't need.

An extremely simple life
during a failure season
is one of the fastest ways
to recover.

When your life becomes simpler,
your soul finally has room
to grow stronger.

14. How to Walk Back From Rock Bottom:

The Rule of Minimal Action

If you are at a low point right now,
remember this:

> Rebirth does not begin
> with a "big decision".
>
> Rebirth almost always starts
> with the smallest actions.
>
> One action per day.
> Do that for thirty days,
> and your reality will begin to change.
>
> For example:
> - Learn something related to your field
> for 10 minutes a day.
> - Reach out to one person per day
> (even just to say hello).
>   - Walk outside a little every day.
>   - Throw away one unnecessary item each day.
>   - Reduce your complaining, even just a bit.
>   - Write down one small plan you'd like to try.
>   - Tidy one corner of your living space each day.
>   - Spend one hour in silence daily.

- Go to bed a little earlier than yesterday.
- Do one small thing

that brings you closer to your future.

These little steps accumulate into strength.

That strength
will pull you back
into the flow of life.

The most dangerous thing
is not failure itself.

The real danger
is staying completely still inside failure.

15. Things You Must Not Do After Failing:

The Most Important Page of Self-Rescue

1. Don't argue, don't defend, don't explain endlessly

The harder you explain after failing,
the more people remember
only one thing:

"You failed."

Silence, in many cases,
is the best protection you have.

2. Don't rush into starting a new business,
reinventing your life, or making huge decisions

Right after failure,
your emotions are murky.

Deciding your future in that state
is like driving in heavy fog.
You might be moving—
but you have no idea where.

3. Don't reach for any kind of anesthesia

Alcohol, drugs,
casual connections,
sweet illusions,
even spiritual or religious rituals
used for pure escapism—

These may delay your breakdown,
but they won't build a foundation
you can stand on.

4. Don't let unimportant people
have power over your emotions

How others see you
will not pay your rent,
and will not live your life for you.

What they say is often
far less important
than you think.

What really matters
is how you move.

5. Don't replay your losses and regrets
over and over in your head

The more you obsess over what you've lost,
the less you can see
what you still have.

16. What True Rebirth Looks Like:

When You Finally Stand on Your Own Side

Rebirth does not begin with victory.

True rebirth begins at the moment
you do one thing:

You stop looking at yourself
from the opposite side of failure,
and instead stand on your own side.

At that moment, you are no longer:
- A victim of the world
- A piece on the chessboard of fate
- A shadow of someone else
- A prisoner of your past

You become someone who:

Can make decisions for yourself.

That is the moment
you truly gain freedom.

17. Conclusion: Success and Failure Are Guests—

You Are the Only Host

Success and failure
are both visitors.

They come to your house,
and they leave.

They bring gifts,
and they bring trouble.

But no matter
how often they come and go,
there is only one person
who has the right to sit
in the host's chair of your life:

That person is you.

When you are no longer intoxicated by success,
and no longer crushed by failure,

you step out of a life
controlled by "results",
and into a life
guided by "awareness".

This Chapter 0
is your starting line.

From the next chapter on,
your real rebirth begins.

Chapter 1 — When You Fail, You Just Fail: Stop Punishing Yourself

Failure is one of the simplest events in life—
and yet, one of the most unbearable for the human heart.

It is simple because it is merely a result.
It is unbearable because we attach too much to that result—
identity, face, pride, future, approval, meaning.

But the most important message of this chapter is this:

> When you fail, you just fail.
> It is nothing more and nothing less.
> No explanation needed. No self-judgment required.
>
> Failure is not fate.
> Failure is not a moral verdict.
> Failure is not the definition of who you are.
> Failure is simply a *state*—a temporary pause on the road.
>
> The real suffering in life does not come from failure itself.
> It comes from the way we treat ourselves after failure happens.

1. Failure Is Not a Philosophical Puzzle You Must "Analyze"

— It is just failure, without deeper meaning

When people fail, the first instinct is to dissect and overthink:
- Where did I go wrong?
- Why did this happen?
- If only I had done X...
- Am I not good enough?
- Does this mean I'll never succeed?
- Is the universe punishing me?

But in reality, most failures have no grand logic.

They do not necessarily mean you made a mistake.
They do not necessarily mean you lacked effort or competence.

Many failures are simply the result of:
- Bad timing
- External environmental shifts
- Someone else's sudden strength
- Insufficient resources
- Three seconds of misunderstanding
- One day of bad luck
- A sudden change in rules
- Someone changing their mind
- Emotion, weather, policy, accidents
- Or simply the turbulence of being alive

In other words:

Failure often has no profound reason.

The mind wants a "perfect explanation"
only because it wants emotional relief.

But the truth is:

Failure is not an object of analysis.
It is an invitation to move forward.

2. Do Not Turn Failure Into a Story About Yourself

— Failure does not mean you are worthless. It means you are moving.

The greatest illusion we fall into is this:

"If I failed, it means I am not good."

But truth is often the opposite.

Failure means only one thing:

You were walking forward.
You were trying.
You were in motion.

The only people who never fail
are the ones who never try.

Failure shows you are alive,
that you are reaching beyond the limits of your past,
that you are stepping toward the future.

Failure is not meant to make you doubt yourself.
Failure is meant to let you *see* yourself.

3. When You Fail, You Just Fail

— No self-punishment. No self-insult.

After failure, most people engage in self-flagellation:
- "I'm so stupid."
- "I always ruin things."
- "I'm hopeless."
- "Maybe I'm not cut out for anything."
- "Look at everyone else compared to me."
- "I have no right to start again."

None of these statements are truths.
They are merely the echoes of a wounded mind.

You are not the failure.
You are simply a human being
who has experienced a failure.

You are not the result.
You are the *person* who had a result.

Failure deserves no shame.
Failure must not be inflated
into a perfect explanation of your entire life.

You stumbled—
that is all.

It is not a life sentence.

4. Regret Is the Biggest Trap Failure Creates

— It chains you to the past and steals your future

Regret is one of the most wasteful and destructive emotions.

Regret does not fix the past.
It does not repair anything.
It does not bring anything back.

Regret only does one thing:

It keeps you still.

But life is always moving forward,
even when you are not.

The more you regret,
the more tightly you lock yourself
inside a prison named "the past."

Remember this:

The true danger is not failure.
The real danger is being stuck in failure.

Failure is a pause,
not a final stop.

5. The Only Meaning of Failure

— It gives you a chance to choose again

Failure is not an ending.
Failure is the entrance to a new beginning.

The single purpose of failure is this:

It forces you to decide:
Do you continue down this road,
or do you choose another one?

Failure is a mirror showing:
- Which relationships never belonged to you
- Which skills need strengthening
- Which habits are hurting you
- Which "dreams" stopped being your dreams long ago
- Which stubbornness is meaningless
- Which efforts were misaligned
- Which direction was never truly yours

If failure never happened,
you would never see these truths.

Failure is not your enemy.
It is your teacher.

6. Do Not Let Failure Bind You

— Failure does not shape your future; your next step does

Failure causes people to freeze,
to shrink back,
to fear the next move.

Thoughts like:

"Maybe I'm not suited for this."
"Maybe I should quit."
"Maybe fate has already decided for me."

But here is the truth:

Failure does not determine your future.
The next step you take determines it.

Life does not change
because you understand everything.

Life changes
because you move.

Your identity is not shaped by how many times you fall,
but by whether you take a step
after you fall.

Strength is not defeating failure.
Strength is:

Walking even after failing.

7. Failure Is the Normal Rhythm of Life

— Success is the exception, not the rule

There is no such thing as a "success without failures."

Every person you admire
walked a path like this:

Failure → Failure → Small success
Failure → Big failure → Next success
Failure → Collapse → Restart → Breakthrough
Failure → Loneliness → Turning point
Failure → Doubt → New beginning → Real success

Success is a rare moment of clarity—
not the usual state of life.

Failure is not abnormal.
Failure is the rhythm of growth.

8. You Do Not Need to Prevent Failure

— You only need to avoid letting failure stay overnight

Failure is not something you avoid forever.
It is something you learn to digest quickly.

Never let failure stay too long.

A sleepless night—fine.
A few days of sadness—normal.

But do not let failure
become your new identity.

Do not let it stay overnight in your soul.

If you fall today,
walk again tomorrow.

Failure is not a burden.
It is simply the sound of landing—
the reminder that:

> You are still someone who can move.

9. At Any Time, You Can Start Again

— Failure cannot take away the one power you always have

Failure can take your money,
your job,
your status,
your opportunities,
your relationships.

But there is one thing
failure can never take:

> Your right to begin again.
>
> As long as you are breathing,
> life offers you infinite chances to restart.
>
> That is the deepest strength
> life has built into its design.

10. Chapter Summary (The Core Sentence)

Remember this:

When you fail, you just fail.

No explanation.
No justification.
No shame.
No regret.
No escape.
No self-blame.

Failure is a moment,
not a lifetime.

Your task is not to "understand failure."
Your task is to walk again.

The sooner you walk,
the sooner life begins moving with you.

Chapter 2 — How to Begin Again:

Reset Your Mind, Take One Action, and That's Enough

After a failure, every person enters a period of inner paralysis.

Nothing feels meaningful.
Nothing feels possible.
The mind is chaotic,
the heart is heavy,
the body feels like lead,
and even breathing feels like a burden.

You know you "should move,"
but you don't know where to start.
You don't know how to start.
You don't even know who you are right now.

This chapter serves one purpose:

> To begin again, you only need ONE action.
> Just one.
>
> Every major turning point in life
> begins with something incredibly small.

1. When you're at your lowest, DO NOT make big plans

— When the emotions are broken, "repair" comes before "running"

The most dangerous moment after a failure
is the urge to reset your whole life overnight.

Breakup → "I'll marry someone else soon."
Business failure → "I'll launch a new company tomorrow."
Losing your job → "I'll move to another country."
Emotional collapse → "I'll change everything."

These impulses feel powerful,
but they're not real power.

They are fear,
disguise as momentum.

When your emotions are damaged,
your judgment will be damaged too.
This is not your weakness—this is biology.

Before you set a new direction,
before you rebuild your future,
you must restore one thing:

> The version of you who can think clearly.

> That is the true beginning.

2. The first step of restarting:

Do ONE thing you can actually do

— The smaller the step, the stronger the effect

Right now, what you need is NOT a "goal."
You need the feeling of movement.

Something that you can do immediately,
something too small to fail.

Examples:
- Clean one corner of your room
- Create a folder named "Future"
- Delete three toxic contacts
- Walk for five minutes
- Watch one short educational video
- Drink something warm
- Write down ONE tiny task
- Send one message that might open a door
- Breathe deeply for one minute
- Throw away one useless item
- Search for a skill you want to learn
- Journal a single sentence

These actions look insignificant,
but each one has power:

They pull you out of paralysis
and back into motion.

The beginning of recovery is not success—
it is movement.

3. Small victories are worth more than big goals

— Your brain needs evidence that you are still capable

After failure, the real pain isn't the result.

It is the belief:

"I'm useless."

That belief kills more dreams than any obstacle.

Big goals only make you freeze.
What you need now is small success:
- Something you can't fail at
- Something simple
- Something achievable today
- Something that proves "I can do things again"

Examples:
- A five-minute walk
- Washing one dish
- Editing one sentence
- Replying to one message
- Organizing one folder

These tiny actions create huge internal change.

They whisper to your brain:

"Look. You can still complete things."
"You are not broken."

"You are returning."

One small step leads to the next,
and soon you are moving again.

4. Every action becomes a stone you throw into your future

— The future isn't designed; it is built by accumulation

People think the future comes from planning.
In reality, the future comes from stacking.
- A short walk → a stone for your health
- One page of study → a stone for your knowledge
- Removing toxic relationships → a stone clearing space
- Five minutes of learning → a stone for new skills
- Cleaning your room → a stone for inner order

Every stone you throw forward
returns someday
as the foundation beneath your feet.

Nothing is wasted.
Every small action becomes:

Future capital.

5. People do not "change suddenly"

— Transformation is not a jump; it's a buildup

After failure, we crave extremes:

"Today I'll change my entire life!"

But real change doesn't happen like that.

Real change follows this sequence:

Small steps → small buildup → small momentum →
sudden jump (but only after enough buildup)

Every visible leap
is the result of long periods of invisible effort.

You don't need to leap.
You only need to walk.

6. What you need is not "courage," but "rhythm"

— Slow is sustainable; slow is powerful

People think recovery requires courage.
But courage is unstable.

What you actually need is rhythm:
- Slow repair
- Slow reorganization
- Slow activity
- Slow return

A consistent rhythm brings your life back to motion.

You don't need to sprint.
You don't need to be brave.
You don't need to be inspired.

Just keep a gentle rhythm.
That alone will rebuild you.

7. Remember: You are NOT starting from zero

Failure tricks people into believing:

"I must start everything over."

But the truth is the opposite.

You are beginning from:
- clarity gained through loss
- insight born from pain
- wisdom filtered through collapse

- lightness from letting things go
- maturity shaped by experience
- a deeper understanding of the world
- a new definition of what matters
- a stronger version of yourself

This is the strongest starting point of your entire life.

You are not starting over.
You are starting with experience.

8. The most important line of this chapter:

"You don't wait for readiness.

Beginning is what creates readiness."

People always say:

"I'll start when I'm ready."

But after failure,
you will NEVER feel ready.

Life does not reward the people who wait.

It rewards the people who start.

Even when afraid.
Even when unsure.
Even when shaky.

Because:

Beginning itself is the preparation.

Once you take the first step,
your mind and body adjust automatically.

Starting is the medicine.
Movement is the cure.

9. Summary:

Restarting simply means moving half a step when you don't want to move

The entire chapter can be summarized in one sentence:

> Restarting =
> moving a tiny bit when your heart says "I can't."
>
> You don't need bravery.
> You don't need a plan.
> You don't need perfection.
>
> You only need one action.
> Small enough to do.
> Small enough to finish.
> Small enough to repeat.
>
> Half a step is enough to restart your life.
>
> Because half a step breaks paralysis—
> and the rest will follow.

Chapter 3— Business Failure & Relationship Failure:
Let Time Wash Them Away

There are two kinds of failures that cut the deepest in a person's life:
the failure of one's work, and the failure of one's love.

Their wounds look different on the surface,
but the cure is the same:

Time.

Not explanation.
Not effort.
Not analysis.
Not justification.
Not trying to win someone back.
Not proving yourself.
Not fighting to hold on.

Just—
letting it flow away.

In this chapter, we explore why the hardest failures in life
must be entrusted to time, not to force.

1. Business failure: what you lose is your "external identity"

When a business collapses,

the most painful loss is not the money.

The real pain is the collapse of a role.

Suddenly, you are no longer:

- the one who stands at the front
- the one who is needed
- the one people rely on
- the one who provides answers
- the one who leads
- the one who knows where they're going
- the one with value and confidence

A part of your "public self" falls apart.

And you start to wonder:

"Am I finished?"

"Maybe I'm not good enough."

"Maybe everything I had was an illusion."

But you must understand:

Your business is only one part of you.

It is not you.

What you lost is the role,

not the person.

The titles, projects, positions, and networks you built

may crumble overnight—

but your experience,

your judgment,

your resilience,

your depth,

your instincts—

none of these can be taken away.

The failure of a business is simply a message telling you:

- This is not the time to expand
- You need to consolidate
- Cash preservation matters more than victory
- Your life should return to its simplest form
- You must stop the bleeding before rebuilding

You are not ending—

you are shutting down temporarily before rebooting.

2. Relationship failure: what you lose is "emotional reliance"

When a relationship ends,

the pain is not really about the person.

The true pain comes from the sudden disconnection

from the emotional system you built around them.

What breaks is:

- the illusion of being understood
- the feeling of being needed
- the imagined future you thought you'd share
- the belief that "we can walk together"
- the habit of having them there
- the emotional safety they provided

You think your world has collapsed—

but in truth:

Only your dependency collapsed.

It is not your worth.

It is not your ability to love.

It is not your future.

Most relationships end simply because:

- your paths split
- your timing changed
- the other person's priorities moved
- your futures no longer overlapped
- emotional compatibility naturally ran out

You cannot control a heart.

Nor can you make someone stay once they've decided to go.

Your job is not to chase,

not to explain,

not to beg,

not to fix.

Your job is simple:

Let time pull you out of the emotional storm.

Time does what tears cannot.

3. If time can wash it away, it was never truly yours

This is a harsh truth,

but one of the most liberating:

Anything that time can take away

was never meant to stay.

What is yours will remain.

What is not yours will fall away.

Time clears three kinds of things:

1. The wrong people

People you once thought you "couldn't live without"?

You'll discover you can—

and life gets lighter.

2. The wrong path

The road you believed was your destiny—
when it collapses,
you'll eventually see
you were never meant to go further down it.

3. The wrong attachments

What you once clung to as if it were everything
will later appear as nothing more than emotional weight.

What time removes
is what life was trying to take away from you.

4. The most important rule after failure:

Do NOT cling

Failure hurts.
But clinging to failure hurts far more.

After business failure, clinging makes you:
- over-explain
- try desperately to prove yourself
- chase the approval of people who no longer care
- hold on to collapsing relationships
- waste your last resources, money, and dignity

After relationship failure, clinging makes you:

- lose yourself
- suffer repeated rejection
- be ignored
- destroy your self-worth
- deepen your wounds
- convince yourself you're unlovable

The most powerful ability after failure is:

Cutting.

No explanations.

No chasing.

No turning back.

You don't need anyone to understand your story.

You don't need to rearrange the past into something beautiful.

You only need one thing:

Let the past stay in the past.

5. The truth you must believe:

"You are still here."

No matter what you lost,

how deeply you hurt,

how shattered your world feels—
You are reading this.

That means:

You are still here.

As long as you are here,
your story is not over.

As long as you are here,
you can rebuild anything.
As long as you are here,
you have another road.

As long as you are here,
life cannot defeat you.

Life continues not because you hold on to the past—
but because you keep walking.

6. Business and relationship failures are not destruction—they are life's "pause button"

A failure is not an ending.
It is a message:

- Your direction needs adjustment
- Your pace needs to slow

- Your life needs reorganization
- Your future needs redesigning
- Your emotions need stillness
- Your heart needs quiet
- Your soul needs fresh air

Failure does not come to crush you.
It comes to stop you.

Because some truths
can only be seen while standing still.
Some pain
can only dissolve in silence.
Some answers
can only be heard in solitude.

7. The ultimate key:

Failure is not something to analyze—
it is something to release

Most people misunderstand failure.

They think failure is for analysis,
for reflection,
for dissecting what went wrong.

But the real truth is:

Failure exists to be released, not dissected.

The more you think about it, the deeper you sink.
The more you replay it, the heavier it becomes.

You are not your failure.
You are simply someone passing through failure.

What failure needs is not analysis.
It needs only one thing:

Time.

Let time strip away the wrong things,
wash away the wrong people,
dissolve the wrong dreams,
and bring new ones.

Your job is not to fight the river.
Your job is:

Let time carry you
toward a brighter shore.

Chapter 4 — Preparing for Failure:

The Philosophy of the Minimum Survival Line

Failure is not an accident in life.
It is not a glitch.
It is not a sign of inadequacy.

Failure is one of the natural seasons of being human.

A truly mature person is not someone who never fails.
A mature person is someone who understands:

> Failure is survivable when you prepare for it.
>
> Failure is inevitable,
> but the destruction caused by failure
> is something you can prevent.
>
> This chapter is not about pessimism.
> It is about one of the most important,
> life-saving forms of wisdom you will ever learn:

The Minimum Survival Line.

You may not control when the storm arrives—
but you can absolutely prepare a foundation
that cannot be blown away.

1. Keeping 12 months of living expenses:

Not caution—dignity

Many people collapse after a failure
not because they lack skill,
not because they lack power,
but because they lack time.

A person without money
is a person without time.

A person without time
is the person most likely to make fatal decisions.

That's why you must remember:

> 12 months of living expenses
> = 12 months of clear thinking
> = 12 months of options
> = 12 months of dignity
> = 12 months of safety

> With this buffer, you will:
> - not panic
> - not choose out of fear
> - not trade your future for the present
> - not sacrifice dignity for survival
> - not destroy yourself trying to appear "okay"

This is more than money.

It is your window of clarity
when everything else collapses.

2. Never borrow high-interest money:

It is drinking poison to quench your thirst

This must be written as an uncompromising rule.

The most dangerous part of failure
is not lacking money.

The danger is what people do
because they lack money:

Borrowing high-interest loans.

High-interest debt is not "borrowing."
It is selling your future life.

High-interest debt will:

- take your future
- destroy your credit
- erode your freedom
- trap you in fear
- drown you in interest
- force you into worse decisions
- eliminate any chance of recovery

Life can be slow.
You can restart many times.
You can fall and rise again.

But high-interest debt—

One mistake will derail your life entirely.

This is the one thing you must never touch.

Ever.

3. Better to let this life break

than destroy the next one

This phrase sounds dramatic,
but it holds an essential truth:

> Your failure must remain contained
> within this chapter of your life—
> you cannot let it poison the next one.

> Life is not a single match.
> Life is a long series of interconnected rounds.

> If you sacrifice:
- your future
- your freedom
- your dignity
- your stability
- your options
- your years

just to save a collapsing situation in the present,
you have truly lost.

The common traps are:
- Pouring all savings into a dying business
- Sacrificing your dignity to save a relationship
- Borrowing heavily to maintain appearances
- Refusing to cut losses
- Making ten bad decisions to defend one mistake

What you need is:

Stop the bleeding—
not continue the damage.

The value of failure is not "fixing it."
The value of failure is knowing where to stop.

Failure should happen once—
not become a chain explosion.

4. Lowering your living costs:

The simpler you live, the stronger you become

During failure, you do NOT need:
- pride
- bravado
- forced optimism
- social image
- unnecessary spending
- emotional performances

You need simplicity.

The rules of failure-period living:
- No smoking
- No drinking
- No gambling
- No drugs

- No unnecessary socializing
- No showing off
- No impulsive purchases
- No new belongings
- No "performing stability" for others

Live quietly.
Live simply.
Shrink your life to the most safe, sustainable form.

Simplicity is not weakness.

Simplicity is your recovery engine.

The quieter your life is,
the stronger you will be.

5. During failure, solitude resets both your body and soul

**When the storm hits,
your job is not to "fight harder."**

Your job is:

Return yourself to the cleanest, most original state.

During failure,
you don't need to perform for anyone.
You don't need to impress anyone.
You don't need to meet any expectation.

A solitary life becomes the fastest way to heal.

The ideal lifestyle during failure:
- regular sleep
- plain food
- rest for the body
- emotional detox
- reduced stimulation
- zero meaningless interactions
- inner quiet

Solitude is not punishment.
Solitude is cleaning.

When your life becomes simple and quiet,
you will finally see yourself again.

6. The true purpose of the minimum survival line:

Protecting your *future abilities*

You might think you are protecting money.
But that is not what you are protecting.

You are protecting:
- your ability to think clearly
- your ability to learn again
- your decision-making capacity
- your power to rebuild
- your emotional endurance
- your ability to face reality
- your will to keep going
- your dignity
- your freedom from fear
- your right to choose your next direction

The minimum survival line exists to ensure:

You do not lose the ability
to succeed again.

7. Preparing for failure

is actually preparing for rebirth

A truly mature person
has these three forms of preparation in place:

1. Financial preparation

One year of safety keeps your mind unbroken.

2. Psychological preparation

Failure is not destruction—
it is restructuring.

3. Life preparation

Knowing that one day,
you will walk forward again.

Failure is not the end.
Failure is the doorway
to your next life chapter.

The minimum survival line is not fear.
It is the foundation of your comeback.

8. If you are in the storm right now,

remember these three sentences

First:

Failure is not what destroys you.
Lack of preparation is.

For the prepared,
failure is a pause.
For the unprepared,
failure is collapse.

Second:

All suffering comes from the fear of shrinking your life.

Knowing when to retreat
is a higher form of strength.

Third:

**The minimum survival line
is an act of kindness toward your future self.**

You are not being pathetic.
You are creating space for rebirth.

9. Summary:

**The minimum survival line is not fear—
it is wisdom**

You cannot stop storms,
but you can strengthen your foundation.

The minimum survival line is:
- understanding life
- respecting the future
- protecting yourself
- taking responsibility for your next chapter

When you learn to prepare for failure,
you have already become someone
who will never truly fall.

Chapter 5 Living Alone:

The Minimalist Way to Rebuild Your Mind and Body

When you fail, what you truly need is not noise, not encouragement, not gatherings, not people telling you to "stay strong."

You need just one thing:

To be alone.

Being alone is not isolation.
Being alone is recovery.

Being alone is not the absence of life.
Being alone is the resetting of life.

Being alone is not emptiness.
Being alone is the space where you rebuild your mind,
your strength,
and your direction.

1. Shrink your life completely: The smaller your life becomes, the faster you recover

After failure, most people rush to create big plans or big goals.

But what you truly need is the opposite:

Make your life as small, gentle, and simple as possible.

When life becomes small,
your mind becomes clear.
Your body becomes lighter.
Your decisions become accurate.

Simplicity is not poverty.
Simplicity is clarity.

Simplicity is not regression.
Simplicity is energy conservation.

Examples:
- Stop buying unnecessary things
- Stop unnecessary socializing
- Stop trying to impress anyone
- Stop doing things only to make others happy
- Stop carrying other people's expectations
- Reduce external input to the absolute minimum

And suddenly you will realize:

You can live with far less than you imagined.

2. Remove all forms of anesthetics:

No smoking, no drinking, no drugs, no "escapes"

After failure, people often reach for "painkillers":

Alcohol to numb the mind.
Cigarettes to numb the nerves.
Drugs to escape the truth.
Casual excitement to avoid loneliness.
Even blind faith or manic positivity becomes a form of escape.

But remember:

Anesthetics delay healing.
They never save you.

They bury the wound,
but they do not close it.

Failure is not something to numb.
Failure is something to awaken from.

You heal faster when you choose clarity over anesthesia.
- No cigarettes
- No alcohol
- No unnecessary medication
- No addictive distractions

Your body must be kept clean,
quiet,
and stable.

This is how you regain real strength.

3. Hide yourself deeply: Build your personal "safety zone"

Being alone is not running away from the world.
It is stepping away from:
- noise
- judgment
- comparison
- pressure
- social performance
- emotional turbulence

You must build a mental safe zone:
- Reduce going out
- See fewer people
- Avoid places that trigger pressure
- Step away from environments of comparison
- Stop explaining yourself to anyone
- Cut off unnecessary relationships

A safety zone is a place where:

No one demands anything from you.
No one judges you.
No one drains your energy.

It is the space where you can breathe again.

Like a plant returning to soil,
you quietly recover.

4. Buy nothing except necessities:

The fastest way to clean the mind is to reduce consumption

Many people shop to fill emotional holes.

Loneliness → buy something.
Stress → buy something.
Fear → buy something.
Restlessness → buy something.

But recovery requires the opposite:

>Reduce external stimulation to near zero
>so the inner world can cleanse itself.

>Once you stop buying, you'll notice:
>- You already have enough
>- Objects cannot heal emotions
>- Consumption is not relief
>- Desire decreases, and the soul becomes lighter

You do not heal by adding more.
You heal by subtracting.

5. Manage your body gently:

Minimal stimulation, maximum recovery

After failure, the body becomes extremely sensitive.

Some people sleep too little,
some sleep too much.
Some eat uncontrollably,
some cannot eat at all.
Some have chest tightness,
some feel heavy limbs,
some burst into tears.

This is normal.

Your task is simple:

>Treat your body with the softest, simplest care.

- Drink a lot of water
- Eat mild, calming foods
- Keep a light, predictable sleep pattern
- Take slow walks
- Avoid late nights
- Reduce caffeine and stimulants
- Rest when your body asks for rest

Your body is your foundation.
Once your body stabilizes,
your mind will follow.

6. Emotional reset:

Quietness is the strongest form of healing

Your emotions after failure are not the enemy.
They are honest signals.

Do not force yourself to be strong.
- If you want to cry, cry.
- If you want silence, stay silent.
- If you don't want to talk, don't talk.
- If you don't want to meet people, don't meet them.
- If you need rest, rest.

Healing begins when emotions flow naturally.

Being alone gives emotions space to breathe.

It is the one environment
where you don't have to wear armor.

7. The purpose of a minimalist life:

To return your mind to a "clean" state

When your life becomes small, silent, and simple—
your inner fog begins to dissolve.

A cleaned mind does not mean the pain disappears.
It means the pain can no longer control you.

A clean mind does not mean isolating from the world.
It means regaining the strength to re-enter it.

Minimalist living gives you three gifts:

1. Sharper perception

You can finally hear your inner voice.

2. Clearer judgment

Without noise, your decisions become accurate.

3. A visible path

Your own, not anyone else's.

Failure is not the end.
Failure is the cleansing of your inner landscape.

8. Being alone is not emptiness—

it is the space where your "real self" returns

In solitude:

People disappear.
Expectations disappear.
Noise disappears.
Comparisons disappear.
Distractions disappear.

And then—
you finally see yourself.

Being alone becomes a mirror:
- What you truly love
- What you actually dislike

- Which relationships drain you
- Which habits suffocate you
- Which dreams were illusions
- Which attachments should be released
- Which direction your heart points to

Everything becomes visible
in the silence.

Solitude is not a void—
it is the birthplace of your original self.

9. Solitude is not to avoid the world—

it is to return to it stronger

Being alone is temporary.
Solitude is training, not exile.

After a period of solitude, a person becomes:
- Less easily shaken
- Less easily pressured
- Less reactive
- Less emotional
- More deliberate
- More grounded
- More stable
- More resilient

Solitude grows inside you a quiet strength.

This is the kind of strength
that withstands any storm.

10. Summary:

Minimalism, solitude, clarity—these are the pillars of rebirth

When you fail, the answer is not to run faster.
The answer is to slow down.

The answer is not to think more.
The answer is to empty the mind.

The answer is not to speak louder.
The answer is to become quiet.

- Shrink your life
- Clean your body
- Calm your emotions
- Protect your space
- Face yourself
- Return to your inner axis
- Rebuild your strength from the inside

This is how you become someone
who can rise again.

This is resilience built from silence.

Chapter 6: Reevaluating Your "Invisible Assets"

— What remains after failure is your true capital

Failure takes many things away.
Money.
Status.
Opportunities.
Relationships.
Certainty.
Identity.
Even the world you thought you owned.

But there is one thing failure cannot take:

>Your foundation — the part of you that survives the storm.

>When the rain washes off all the external layers,
>whatever remains standing
>is your real asset.

>This chapter helps you identify,
>clarify,
>and reclaim
>those invisible assets —
>the ones that will rebuild your next life chapter.

1. Failure removes "external power,"

but strengthens the "power that comes from within"

When life is smooth,
we confuse external support with our own strength.

Success gives you many kinds of borrowed power:
- Confidence supported by praise
- Value supported by income
- Security supported by relationships
- Identity supported by titles
- A false sense of fullness supported by busyness

But the moment failure arrives,
these borrowed powers disappear.

You may think:

"I've lost everything."

But what you lost
was external scaffolding —
not your real strength.

What failure cannot take:
- Your judgment
- Your knowledge
- Your skills
- Your thinking patterns
- Your experience
- Your resilience
- Your observation
- Your sensitivity to the world
- Your accumulated insight
- The wisdom you extracted from pain

These are not shaken by storms.
These are your true assets.

2. After failure, the first task is not regret —

it is "inventory."

Inventory does not mean counting money.
Money is surface-level.

"Real inventory" means checking:
1. your abilities
2. your relationships
3. your unique strengths

This is your starting point.

1. What can you still do?

Your skills did not disappear.
- Skills you have trained
- Projects you've completed
- Industries you understand
- Abilities your body remembers
- Things you can do without hesitation
- Knowledge that took years to accumulate

Failure empties your bank account,
but it does not empty your abilities.

2. Who remains in your circle? (Your "gold" connections)

Failure reveals the truth of relationships.

The people who stay:
- Those who still pick up your calls
- Those who will listen
- Those who offer advice
- Those who are willing to introduce opportunities
- Those who treat you the same in low times
- Those who don't judge your temporary state

These are your real network.

A network is not about quantity.
It is about the people who remain
when you have nothing to offer.

3. What unique advantages do you have that others don't?

This is one of the most important questions:

What do you have that cannot be replicated?

Examples:
- Deep experience in a specific industry
- Intuition built from years of exposure

- Technical knowledge others don't have
- Insight into certain types of customers
- Understanding of specific materials, processes, or supply chains
- Knowledge of markets that others cannot enter
- Experiences others have never lived through
- The ability to solve a certain type of problem

These are differentiating assets.
Often more valuable than you realize.

3. Expand your market:

**The issue is often not "no value,"
but "the wrong pond."**

After a failure, people often think:

"I'm worthless now."

But the truth is usually:

Your value didn't disappear —
you were simply in the wrong environment.

The same ability can be:
- Ordinary in one industry
- Highly valued in another
- Invisible in one market
- Essential in another
- Common in one country
- Rare in another

Sometimes your talent is not the problem —
your location is.

The key after failure is:

Expand your market.
Change the environment.

Never stay where your value is invisible.

4. Rebuild your connections:

Take everything — large or small — without pride

Pride is the most dangerous enemy during a low point.

What you need now is not "status,"
but momentum.
- Take small jobs
- Take simple tasks
- Take introductions, favors, and opportunities
- Reconnect with old contacts
- Build new ones
- Accept imperfect options
- Say yes to work that aligns with your skills
- Avoid saying, "This is too small for me."

You're not trying to prove anything right now.
You are rebuilding your base.

In a rebuilding phase:

Everything that increases your cash flow,
your experience,
or your network —
is valuable.

The worst thing you can do in a low point
is to be picky.

5. Your "special product knowledge" is often worth more than your résumé

Your résumé is limited.
It cannot express your real expertise.

But your accumulated product knowledge has enormous value:
- Understanding certain materials
- Knowledge of specific production processes
- Sensitivity to certain types of customers
- Familiarity with niche markets
- Deep experience with supply chains

- Industry intuition
- Years of "invisible training" you lived through

These are "hidden strengths."

You might not even notice them —
but they are powerful assets that others don't have.

6. After failure, your greatest weapon is your ability to learn again

Failure is not a punishment.
Failure is an update notification.

The strongest comeback is never money.
It is learning.
- Learn a skill that can bring income
- Learn a new tool
- Learn a new market
- Learn a field you avoided before
- Upgrade old abilities into modern versions
- Learn one thing every day

Knowledge cannot be taken from you.

Learning is the shortest path back to strength.

7. What you need after failure isn't luck —

it's "redefining yourself."

The most important reconstruction after failure is not financial.
It is identity reconstruction.

Your external labels may be gone —
but your direction can be chosen.

Ask yourself:
- Who do I want to become now?
- Which direction do I want to walk?
- Which abilities will I keep?

- Which habits will I abandon?
- Which relationships are worth rebuilding?
- Which industries offer better opportunities for me?
- What kind of life do I want to design from here?

Failure resets your identity.

And that's a gift —
you can start fresh.

8. In the end, failure is not "zeroing out."

Failure is "filtering."

Failure removes:
- Fake friends
- Wrong industries
- Useless habits
- Unsuitable dreams
- Hollow identities
- Borrowed confidence
- External noise

But failure keeps:
- Your real skills
- Your real experience
- Your real judgment
- Your real resilience
- Your real network
- Your real insight
- Your real strength
- Your real will to rise again

Failure does not mean "I have nothing left."
Failure means:

"Now I finally see what truly belongs to me."

Chapter 7: Relearning: Rebuilding Yourself Through Books, Skills, and Buddhist Wisdom

— Mature people save themselves through learning

When a person falls, the strongest counterattack is not money,
not motivation,
not a pep talk,
not someone's encouragement,
not a miracle.

It is one thing:

> Learning again.

> Learning is the most loyal tool in your low point—
> it is cheap,
> quiet,
> patient,
> and never betrays you.

> Everything you learn in the lowest days of your life
> will return to save you somewhere in the future.

> This chapter is about rebuilding your thinking,
> your skills,
> your emotional foundation,
> your perspective,
> and ultimately your path—
> from the inside out.

1. Mature people rise not through emotion, but through learning

When we're young, we fight with impulse and emotion.
Pain appears → we escape, we numb, we force our way through.

But anyone who has lived long enough learns this simple truth:

> After collapse, the only reliable restart is learning.

> Why?

Because learning is:
- The most stable form of growth
- The most certain way to rise again
- The investment no one can steal
- The resource nobody can cut off
- The long-term asset that compounds silently

Failure creates chaos.
Learning creates order.

Failure brings self-doubt.
Learning brings self-recognition.

Failure stops your life.
Learning restarts it.

2. After failure, why learning must come before money

Most people fall and think:

"I need to make money right now."

But the more you rush,
the more you lose.

Why?

Because right after a major failure,
you are in the worst state for financial decisions:
- Your emotions are unstable
- Your judgment is cloudy
- Your perspective is narrow
- Your direction is unclear
- Your inner compass is shaking
- The world around you has changed
- Your old methods no longer work

Chasing money in this condition
almost guarantees a second failure.

Money is a result.

Learning is a cause.

Without fixing the cause,
the result will not change.

Learning stabilizes you.
It strengthens your mind,
sharpens your vision,
widens your options,
and rebuilds your confidence
from within.

When you are ready—
money naturally follows.

3. Where does relearning begin? Three pathways

Relearning does not require returning to school.
It does not require pressure or strict discipline.

It begins with three gentle doors:

Path 1 — Books: updating the "operating system" of your mind

You don't read to become smarter.
You read to become clearer.

Books allow you to:
- Borrow other people's mistakes
- See the structure of the world
- Learn from decades of knowledge in days
- Expand your emotional vocabulary
- Build a calm and stable inner world
- Understand human nature and history
- Strengthen professional depth

A book is a temporary replacement brain.
One book adds one perspective.
Ten books add ten lives.
Fifty books change your mental architecture.

What to read after failure?
- History (people never change)
- Business (judgment improves)
- Psychology (you stabilize)
- Biographies (learn how others stood back up)
- Professional books (build future income)

Books are the quietest medicine for a wounded heart.

Path 2 — Skills: building new options for your future

After failure, your biggest loss is not money—
it's options.

Skill learning restores those lost options.

You can learn:
- Coding
- Design
- Marketing
- Languages
- Industry-specific knowledge
- Manufacturing and supply chains
- Data analysis
- Writing
- Communication
- Product development
- Business models
- Any tool that works in your profession

Skills are the fastest way to produce value again.

Path 3 — Buddhist teachings: rebuilding the axis of the heart

Your sentence captures the spirit of this chapter:

"When you fail, don't cling to Buddha — find your true self."

Profound.
Accurate.

Universal.

Buddhism is not for escape.
It is a mirror.

It helps you:
- See the root of your pain
- Understand attachment
- Calm emotion
- Regain clarity
- Let go of unnecessary desires
- Observe your mind without judgment
- Ask the real "Why am I suffering?"

Buddhism does not save you.
It teaches you to save yourself.

Not by kneeling,
not by begging,

but by understanding.

4. Why learning during your low point becomes five times more powerful

Because during failure:
- Your ego is thin
- Your mental noise is low
- You are forced to face reality
- Your heart is open
- Your attention is sharp
- Your desire for transformation is strong

People rarely learn deeply when life is smooth.
Pleasure makes the mind dull.

But failure makes the mind crystal clear.

Low points are the most fertile soil for growth.

5. The purpose of relearning is not to "be strong"

but to be stable

Strength is temporary.
Stability is eternal.

Learning gives you:
- Less panic
- Less comparison
- Less emotional reaction
- Less overthinking
- Less impulsive decision-making
- More accurate judgment
- More emotional calmness
- More long-term patience

Stability is the true adult power.

6. What you learn today will save you somewhere in the future
- A sentence you read today may save a decision next month
- A skill you learn now may open a door next year
- A concept you understand now may protect your relationships later
- A habit you rebuild now will shape your decade

In life,
no learning is wasted.

Everything returns.
Everything compounds.

7. Relearning is not returning to who you were —

it is becoming the upgraded version of yourself

Failure is not destruction;
it is evolution.

Relearning is not restoration;
it is renewal.

Every chapter you read,
every skill you practice,
every insight you absorb,
moves you closer to the next version of yourself:
- Higher perspective
- Deeper thinking
- Sharper judgment
- More stable emotions
- Cleaner inner world
- More solid expertise
- Wiser relational boundaries

Upgraded you
won't repeat the old mistakes.
Upgraded you
doesn't live on luck.
Upgraded you
cannot be easily shaken.

8. The conclusion: learning is the strongest counterattack of the fallen

When you fall, you don't need:
- Speed
- Excuses
- Explanations
- Revenge
- Others' approval
- Sudden success

You need one thing:

Learning.

Learning never betrays you.
Learning never leaves you.
Learning is the only power
that grows even when everything else collapses.

Every time you learn,
you move half a step forward.

When those half-steps accumulate,
you look back
and realize—

You have already rebuilt yourself.

Chapter 8 — Rebuilding the Way You Live: Living Calm and Unmoved

— Solitude is the period when your character is reborn

The tone is faithful to the Chinese and Japanese versions, refined for English-language readers with a natural, literary flow.

Chapter 8: Rebuilding the Way You Live: *Living Calm and Unmoved*
— Solitude is the time when a person's character is rebuilt

After failure, collapse, separation, loss, and isolation,
the first thing that begins to shake
is not your career,
not your finances,
not even your lifestyle.

It is your "way of being."
How you react.
How you think.
How you stand.
How you face the world.
How you treat people.
How you treat yourself.

Solitude is like a quiet, spacious dressing room.
Inside it, you finally have the room to take off your old personality
and put on a new one that truly belongs to you.

This chapter is about how, in solitude,
you rebuild your way of being—
how you become quiet, grounded, steady, clear—
and become a person even you can respect.

1. After failure, a person's personality naturally begins to "loosen"

When life is smooth, your personality becomes rigid.
You don't question yourself.
You don't reflect.
You don't notice blind spots.

But the moment you fall into a valley,
your personality begins to loosen at the edges:
- pride softens
- reactions slow
- unnecessary fixations crumble
- dependency weakens
- fears become visible
- emotional reflexes appear in the light

Most people panic and say,
"Why am I becoming so fragile?"

But the truth is:

Fragility is not a breakdown.
It is the beginning of becoming flexible.

Just as a house cannot be renovated without breaking some walls,
a person cannot be rebuilt without loosening the old shell.

When you see your own weakness clearly,
you are not falling apart—
you are preparing for renewal.

2. The deeper the valley, the more you must learn to become "a steady person"

Steadiness is not pretending to be strong.
It is not suppressing emotion.
It is not gritting your teeth.

Steadiness is a quiet inner stance—
a refusal to be dragged or shaken by small things.

A steady person:
- does not rush to explain
- does not rush to defend
- does not rush to argue
- does not rush to react
- does not rush to prove
- does not rush to judge
- does not rush to make conclusions

A steady person:
- is not toppled by small nonsense
- is not inflated by praise
- is not crushed by failure
- is not controlled by others
- is not ruled by emotion
- knows their own pace

Steadiness is a strength born only in solitude.

3. Don't listen to slander. Don't argue. Don't explain. Protect your energy.

When you fall, many voices appear:
- gossip
- criticism
- misunderstanding
- judgment
- unasked-for advice
- quiet mockery
- disguised pity

In the past, you might have rushed to clarify.
To defend yourself.
To correct others.
To prove your innocence.

But now you must understand:

Explanation is a luxury for the insecure.
Argument is the trap that destroys people in recovery.

The more you explain,
the more powerless you look.

The more you argue,
the more you give unwanted people control over your life.

So you learn three simple replies:

"I understand."
"It's alright."

"Thank you."

Then you close the door.

You do not need to win the debate.
You need to win your life.

4. Solitude is your chance to "clear out" the unnecessary

Once you enter solitude, you begin to see with surprising clarity.

You start deleting:
- pointless relationships
- friendships built on convenience
- people who use you
- affection that never returns
- promises that only exhaust you
- unwanted social pressure
- ego-driven comparison
- cluttered habits
- invisible obligations
- self-betrayal disguised as "kindness"

Solitude is not the absence of people—
it is the removal of the wrong ones.

It is a deep cleansing.
It is a reset.
It is a purification of your inner space.

What remains after solitude
is what truly belongs in your life.

5. Learn "calm and unmoved":

Unaffected by storms outside, unshaken by waves inside

Calm and unmoved does not mean coldness.
It does not mean detachment.
It does not mean apathy.

It means:
the world may shake, but you remain steady.

It means:
- you hear outer noise but are not pulled by it
- you feel emotion but are not ruled by it
- you see people but do not lose yourself in them
- you walk at your own pace
- you choose your goals
- you decide your direction
- your inner compass is stronger than outer pressure

This state cannot be obtained in crowds.
Only in solitude does it begin to grow.

6. Solitude is the golden period of character reconstruction

In solitude, your real priorities become obvious:
- Who am I living for?
- What have I been clinging to?
- Which desires were real?
- Which goals were illusions?
- What do I truly value?
- What must I finally let go of?

Solitude reorganizes your entire inner world.

In solitude, you will:
- drop other people's expectations
- identify false dreams
- silence external noise
- start learning again
- rebuild your standards
- refine your values
- regain your axis
- return to your true self

Solitude is not empty.
Solitude is formative.
It is the workshop where your next version is forged.

7. Mature people always look "as if nothing is happening"

Even in chaos,
mature people remain composed.

Their heart may be shaking,
but their steps are steady.

They:
- do not panic
- do not shout
- do not exaggerate
- do not compare
- do not collapse
- do not dramatize
- do not let small things disturb them

This is not repression.
It is discipline.
It is personal mastery.

Those who walk quietly, walk the farthest.
Those who stand calmly, stand the strongest.

8. Conclusion:

**Solitude does not make you harder.
It makes you steadier.**

Many people think strength comes from "becoming harder."

But hard things break.
Steady things endure.

Solitude does not turn you into a stone.
Solitude turns you into a tree.

A tree is quiet.
A tree is deep.
A tree is grounded.
A tree bends with the wind but does not fall.

Solitude teaches you to live like a tree:
calm, rooted, stable, unshakable.

Until you can live this way,
solitude continues to strengthen you.

That is the true power of solitude.

Chapter 9 — Keep Moving in Your Field:

The World Belongs to Those Who Take Action

Even if you have fallen, even if you're lost, even if you're alone —
there is only one thing you must not do: stop.

There is one truth in life that never betrays:

The world always opens its doors to those who keep moving.

You may fail.
You may lose everything.
You may be exhausted, rejected, embarrassed, forgotten.
You may stand alone with no resources, no direction, no confidence.

But no matter what happens,
you must not stand still.

Two months of stopping won't hurt you.
Six months of stopping pushes you from "inside" to "outside."
One year of stopping makes you a "forgotten person."
Three years of stopping makes you a stranger even to yourself.

This chapter tells you one thing:

The world never abandons a person who continues to move.

1. Why must a failed person never stop?

Because stopping is the real death.

Failure is not deadly.
Stopping is.

Losing direction isn't fatal.
Losing the ability to act is.

You don't need to know your next step.
You don't need goals.

You don't need plans.
You don't need clarity.

You need movement.

Life does not change because you think.
Life changes because you move.

We do not act once we understand.
We understand only after we act.

2. Why keep moving?

Because opportunity lies on the road, not in your home.

Opportunity will not ring your doorbell.
Luck will not phone you.
The market will not wait until you're "ready."

The world only reveals itself to:

people who are already on the move.

Walk through a factory and you'll see what others can't.
Walk through a trade show and you'll hear what others can't.
Visit clients, talk to colleagues, study competitors, go to the field —
you will collide with people and information
that would never appear if you stayed still.

You may feel like you are wandering without a direction,
but every step is creating unseen possibilities.

Opportunity is never found by waiting.
Opportunity is created by moving into it.

3. Your lowest point is often the moment

when others finally "see" who you really are

You might think:

"Who would pay attention to me now?"

But you are wrong.

The people who have truly succeeded in life
know exactly what it feels like to start from zero.

When you are in the valley, they observe you more carefully.

If you:
- keep walking
- keep learning
- keep showing up
- keep trying
- keep breathing even with pain

they quietly think:

"This person will rise again."

But if you pretend to be fine, pretend to be successful,
pretend to be above your circumstances —
those same people will never help you.

Your sincerity in your darkest stage
is more powerful than any performance in your brightest stage.

People who work hard recognize each other instantly.

4. Moving in your profession is a stronger weapon than any degree

Real expertise today comes not from certificates,
but from being actively present in your field.

True professional power comes from three actions:

(1) Move

Go. Walk. Visit. Observe. Show up.
Information becomes real only when your feet touch the ground.

(2) See

There are countless things you will never notice on a screen:
- production
- materials
- quality
- logistics
- costs
- customer behavior
- defects
- market changes
- silent trends

Seeing gives you understanding.
Understanding gives you judgment.

(3) Sense

Industries have a smell.
Materials have a smell.
Nations have a smell.
Trends have a smell.

Only those who show up in person
can sense whether something is about to rise or fall.

This sense is impossible to acquire from articles or reports.

It is earned only by moving.

5. The more you move, the more irreplaceable you become

Most people hide behind screens and information.

Only a few stand where reality happens.

And reality has a rule:

People who go to the field
are always more valuable
than those who remain in the office.

As you continue to move, you will naturally become someone who:
- understands customers deeply
- reads the market accurately
- grasps industry structure
- senses risk early
- connects the supply chain
- sees the essence beneath the surface

Eventually, people begin to say:

"Things move faster when you arrive."
"Problems disappear when you show up."

This kind of value does not vanish even after failure.
It is the kind of value that rebuilds your life.

6. Meeting people is the fastest way to reopen your life

You don't need to meet a hundred people.
One is enough.

One person can shift your direction.
One conversation can change your perspective.
One handshake can open an industry.
One introduction can rewrite your future.

This is why you must go out.
Because:

To meet people is to meet new worlds.

And those worlds are never inside your home.
They are always on the road.

7. Movement is the most accurate GPS for life direction

Life direction does not come from thinking.
It comes from walking.

Walk one step — you receive feedback.

Walk another — a new clue appears.

Even if you walk the wrong way,
movement allows you to correct.

But the moment you stop,
your map disappears.

Direction is not something you discover first.
Direction is something that reveals itself
to those who are already walking.

8. Only those who "smell the world" can find new opportunities

The world changes faster than you imagine.
Trends shift quietly.
Industries rise and collapse under the surface.
Prices fluctuate.
Nations awaken or decline.

Only those who keep moving
can smell:
- a country becoming suddenly cost-competitive
- a material exploding in demand
- a region gaining policy advantage
- an industry beginning to die
- an old sector quietly reviving

Opportunities do not present themselves as announcements.
They appear first as a faint smell
that only the moving can detect.

9. Trade shows are crossroads of destiny

A trade show is not "a place to look at products."
A trade show is
a place where lives change.

At a trade show, you:
- feel the speed of the world

- see the pulse of global industries
- connect with key players
- discover collaborations
- expand your worldview
- sharpen your intuition
- redesign your future

Ten trade shows
will advance you farther
than three years of thinking at home.

Trade shows are where the world moves.
Walk through them, and your internal compass resets.

10. The world always rewards those who keep moving

You can be slow.
You can be uncertain.
You can be awkward.
You can be afraid.
You can be alone.

Just don't stop.

The world does not favor the smartest,
or the most talented,
or the richest,
or the most connected.

The world favors:

the one who keeps walking.

Walk — and someone will eventually notice you.
Walk — and opportunities will begin to approach.
Walk — and life will begin to move again.

Because:

The world is always in motion.
If you take one step,
the world takes one step toward you.

Chapter 10 — Silence Is Gold: The Final Lesson of Rebirth

Silence is not escape.
Silence is the moment when your power returns to your body.

When a person falls into a low point,
the true danger is not the failure itself.

The danger is:

the collapse of emotions,
and the collapse of words.

Emotional collapse harms you.
Verbal collapse harms your future.

Rebirth has many stages—
clearing, letting go, learning, healing, taking small steps—
but the last and most crucial lesson is only one:

Can you become quiet?

Silence is the graduation exam of rebirth.

1. The darker the period, the less you should speak

When you stumble, the world suddenly becomes loud:
- Curiosity
- Hidden mockery
- Superficial sympathy
- Rumors behind your back
- "Advice" you never asked for
- People trying to peek into your weakness

The more you explain,
the more people think you're making excuses.

The more you defend yourself,
the more desperate you appear.

The more you argue,
the more unstable you seem.

You think you're clarifying,
but what others see is your struggle.

When you are in your lowest valley,
your words lose weight—
but your silence gains power.

Silence is the one weapon that never backfires.

2. Silence is not weakness—it is the refusal to outsource your worth

Anxious people talk too much.
Fear makes people explain themselves endlessly.

But the truly strong behave differently.

Those who can stay silent
have already placed their worth within themselves.

They do not need outside approval.
They do not need others to hold up their pride.
They do not need to "prove" anything with words.

Silence is the act of retrieving your value
from other people's hands
and placing it back into your own.

3. Silence protects the future version of you

In low periods, your judgment becomes cloudy:
- Emotions are too raw
- Thoughts too scattered
- Pride too fragile
- Reactions too impulsive
- Words too emotional

Anything you say now

will become a burden later.

Words spoken in pain today
can become chains around your feet tomorrow.

Silence protects
the you who will have to deal with the consequences.

4. Not everyone deserves to hear your truth

Loneliness reveals people's true colors:
- Some care
- Some pretend to care
- Some observe
- Some judge
- Some quietly enjoy your downfall
- Some use your moment as gossip
- Some only want information

The more you open your heart,
the more you are consumed.

Silence draws a line:

Your heart is not a public square.
Your vulnerability is not anyone's entertainment.

Only a few people in your life
deserve access to your truth.

5. Silence becomes the cleanest filter for relationships

When you stop:
- Explaining
- Justifying
- Complaining
- Proving yourself
- Broadcasting your pain

You notice something surprising:

Only two kinds of people remain:

those who truly care,
and those who truly matter.

Everyone else
disappears naturally.

Silence purifies your world.

6. Silence helps you regain control of your life

When you stop reacting—
people lose their ability to manipulate your emotions.

When you stop explaining—
they can no longer twist your narrative.

When you stop revealing—
they lose access to your weaknesses.

Silence is strength.
Silence lets you reclaim the steering wheel of your life.

Closing your mouth
is sometimes the fastest way
to reclaim your direction.

7. Silence pulls your scattered energy back into yourself

The more you talk,
the more your energy leaks outward.

The more you remain silent,
the more that energy returns to you.

Silence restores:
- Balance
- Focus
- Judgment

- Pace
- Boundaries
- Independence
- Inner tension and strength

Silence is the ritual
of letting your power return home.

Your energy begins to gather again—
quietly, steadily, deeply.

8. Silence is the fastest way to rebuild true confidence

When you become quiet,
you finally hear:
- your own voice
- your own reasoning
- your real desires
- your hidden fears
- the truth you've been avoiding

In silence,
your thinking clears,
your emotions settle.

Silence is a system reboot
for the mind and soul.

And from this quietness
comes a confidence that does not depend on applause,
but is born from clarity.

9. Silence is preparation for your next rise

Silence is not the end—
silence is storage.

During silence, you are actually:
- resting
- healing

- rebuilding
- reorganizing
- filtering
- observing
- realigning
- storing strength

Silence is contraction before expansion.
Silence is crouching before a leap.

Once silence has fully ripened,
you will rise again
in a completely different form.

10. Silence is the mark of strength and the signature of maturity

The more one grows,
the quieter one becomes.

The wiser one becomes,
the less one needs to speak.

Truly strong people:
- do not argue
- do not explain
- do not show off
- do not seek validation
- do not expose their weakness to strangers
- do not let others' opinions dictate their direction

Silence is adulthood.
Silence is wisdom.
Silence is armor.

Only people who can be silent
are qualified to speak powerfully.

Epilogue — After silence, a new life begins

Once you master silence,
your rebirth is complete.

You are no longer:
- manipulated by others
- hijacked by emotions
- trapped by the past
- enslaved by opinions

You become:
- calm
- deep
- steady
- clear
- independent
- grounded
- free

After silence,
you return to the world—
stronger, quieter, sharper.

Your next life begins
from this stillness.

Epilogue — May You Meet Yourself Again in the Quiet

To question is the final dignity of being human.
When a society learns again to doubt, to reflect, and to record,
it regains its soul.
And the same is true for an individual.

When you sit in solitude and quietly ask yourself:

"Who am I?
Is the path I'm walking truly mine?
Where do I wish to go from here?"

your life begins to light up again.

Loneliness is not punishment.
Loneliness is a door.
You think it locks you in the dark,
but it is really shutting out the noise
so you can finally hear your own voice.

You believed loneliness was taking something from you,
but loneliness was giving you
a place to grow your strength again.

1. Everything you have lived through was not meant to make you bitter—it was meant to wake you up

Failure is not an ending.
Loss is not a sentence.
Loneliness is not the last page of your story.

These things did not come to destroy you.
They came to reveal something you long avoided:
the part of yourself that is real.

Here is the hardest truth of life:

No one can live your life for you.
No one can carry your pain for you.

When you fall, you must stand up on your own.
When the night is dark, you must walk by yourself.
In silence, you must learn how to heal.

But here is life's gentlest truth:

Your truest strength appears only when you are alone.

When every external support fades,
you finally realize—
you are far more capable
than you ever imagined.

2. You don't need to win in anyone else's eyes—you only need to walk your own path

After reading this book,
you are beginning to understand:

Life is not something given by others,
and it is not something decided by others.

For so long you were compared,
expected, shaped, defined, judged,
and pushed into the standards of someone else's world.

But the road ahead
can belong to you alone.

You don't need to please anyone.
You don't need to prove anything.
You don't need to become the version others want.
You don't even need to become a "successful person."

You only need to become someone who:

does not lose themselves in the noise.

The moment you stop living by other people's voices,
you have already won.

3. Loneliness is not emptiness—it is space where new life can grow

You were forced to let go of many things:

Relationships, work, beliefs, habits, identities, dependencies...

At that time, you suffered.
You were angry.
You were heartbroken.
It felt like everything was being taken away.

But now you can see:

Most of what you "lost"
were things that had already outgrown your life.

Loneliness emptied you
so that something new could enter:
- A new perspective
- New inner strength
- A calmer pace
- Deeper relationships
- A renewed dream
- A clearer direction

Loneliness does not hollow you out.
Loneliness makes room for growth.

4. In silence, you grow a steadier, heavier, unshakable soul

The person you are now
is no longer the one who relied on noise,
approval,
or external validation to feel alive.

You have learned:
- Not to rush
- Not to fear
- Not to raise your voice
- Not to argue
- Not to explain

- Not to flaunt
- Not to please

You have learned to be quiet.
You have learned to be with yourself.
You have learned to slow down.
You have learned to stand beside yourself.
You have learned to hold your own strength.

Your heart is deeper.
Your judgment sharper.
Your soul heavier, grounded, steady.

You are no longer
someone the wind can blow away.

5. With the strength you grew in solitude, you will walk back into the world again

Loneliness is not a retreat from the world.
Loneliness is training—
a place to gather new power
so you can return to the world with clarity.

When you step out again, you will be different:
- Noise won't move you
- Emotions won't sweep you away
- A single comment won't shake you
- You won't bend yourself to prove worth
- Fake relationships won't trap you
- New beginnings won't scare you

You return as someone
who can stand on your own feet—
calm, grounded, steady.

Final Blessing

When you close this book,
I hope you can gently tell yourself:

"I did not lose.
I am simply beginning again."

Do not fear loneliness.
It is a gift from life—
a place, a time, a silence
given only to those who are ready to grow.

May you, in that silence,
meet the real you once more.

May you walk your own road
from this moment on.

May you be peaceful,
clear-minded,
free,
and quietly strong.

And may you—
again and again—
rise anew from here.